HAL•LEONARD®

BASS
PLAY-ALONG

AUDIO
ACCESS
INCLUDED

STEELY DAN

PLAYBACK+
Speed • Pitch • Balance • Loop

To access audio visit:
www.halleonard.com/mylibrary

Enter Code
6312-6427-4903-8328

Photo: © John Atashian / Retna Ltd.

ISBN 978-1-4234-3212-8

7777 W. BLUEMOUND RD. P.O. BOX 13819 MILWAUKEE, WI 53213

Visit Hal Leonard Online at
www.halleonard.com

HAL•LEONARD® BASS PLAY-ALONG

AUDIO ACCESS INCLUDED

STEELY DAN

VOL. 19

CONTENTS

Bass Notation Legend

Bass music can be notated two different ways: on a *musical staff*, and in *tablature*

THE MUSICAL STAFF shows pitches and rhythms and is divided by bar lines into measures. Pitches are named after the first seven letters of the alphabet.

TABLATURE graphically represents the bass fingerboard. Each horizontal line represents a string, and each number represents a fret.

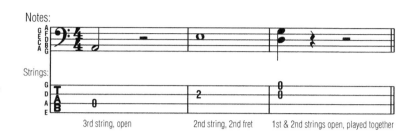

3rd string, open   2nd string, 2nd fret   1st & 2nd strings open, played together

HAMMER-ON: Strike the first (lower) note with one finger, then sound the higher note (on the same string) with another finger by fretting it without picking.

PULL-OFF: Place both fingers on the notes to be sounded. Strike the first note and without picking, pull the finger off to sound the second (lower) note.

LEGATO SLIDE: Strike the first note and then slide the same fret-hand finger up or down to the second note. The second note is not struck.

SHIFT SLIDE: Same as legato slide, except the second note is struck.

TRILL: Very rapidly alternate between the notes indicated by continuously hammering on and pulling off.

TREMOLO PICKING: The note is picked as rapidly and continuously as possible.

VIBRATO: The string is vibrated by rapidly bending and releasing the note with the fretting hand.

SHAKE: Using one finger, rapidly alternate between two notes on one string by sliding either a half-step above or below.

NATURAL HARMONIC: Strike the note while the fret hand lightly touches the string directly over the fret indicated.

MUFFLED STRINGS: A percussive sound is produced by laying the fret hand across the string(s) without depressing them and striking them with the pick hand.

BEND: Strike the note and bend up the interval shown.

BEND AND RELEASE: Strike the note and bend up as indicated, then release back to the original note. Only the first note is struck.

RIGHT-HAND TAP: Hammer ("tap") the fret indicated with the "pick-hand" index or middle finger and pull off to the note fretted by the fret hand.

LEFT-HAND TAP: Hammer ("tap") the fret indicated with the "fret-hand" index or middle finger.

SLAP: Strike ("slap") string with right-hand thumb.

POP: Snap ("pop") string with right-hand index or middle finger.

Additional Musical Definitions

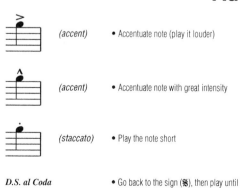

(accent) • Accentuate note (play it louder)

(accent) • Accentuate note with great intensity

(staccato) • Play the note short

D.S. al Coda • Go back to the sign (%), then play until the measure marked *"To Coda"*, then skip to the section labelled *"Coda."*

Fill • Label used to identify a brief pattern which is to be inserted into the arrangement.

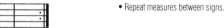

• Repeat measures between signs.

• When a repeated section has different endings, play the first ending only the first time and the second ending only the second time.

Deacon Blues

Words and Music by Walter Becker and Donald Fagen

They got a name for the win-ners in the world, I want a name when I lose. They

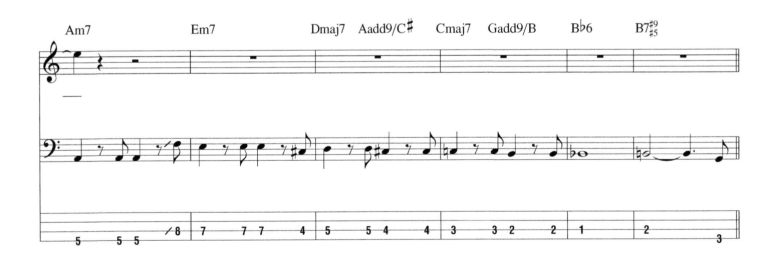

call Al - a - bam - a the Crim - son Tide, call me Dea - con Blues.

Saxophone Solo

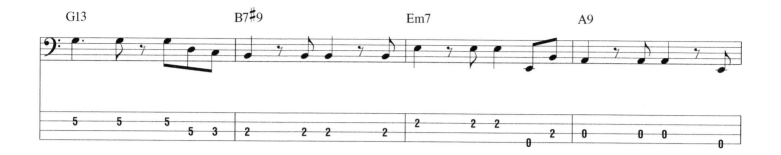

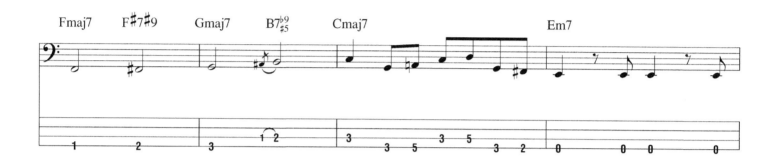

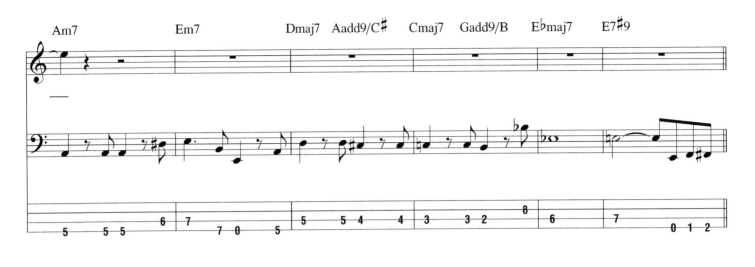

Outro

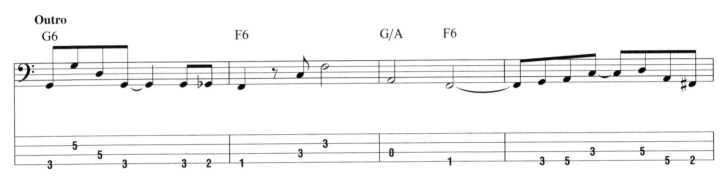

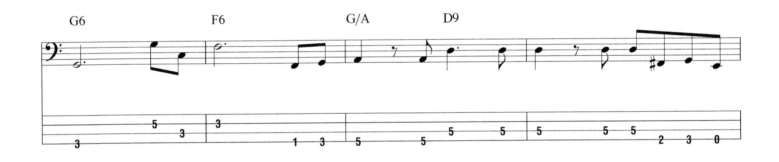

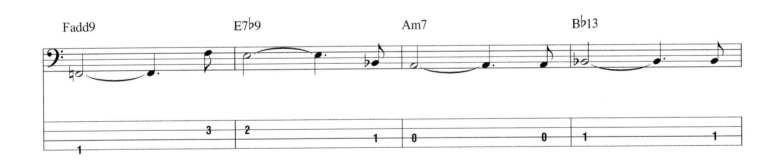

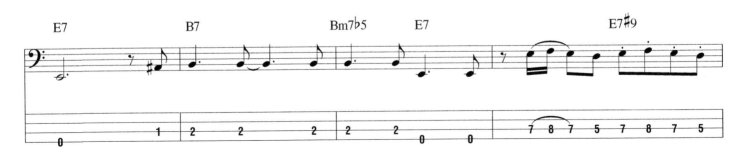

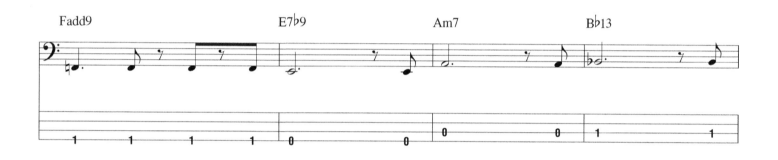

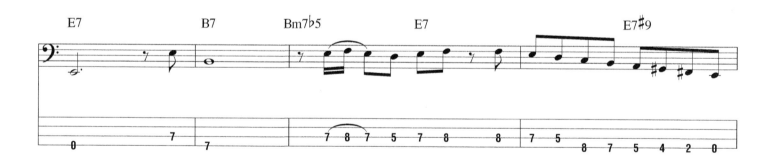

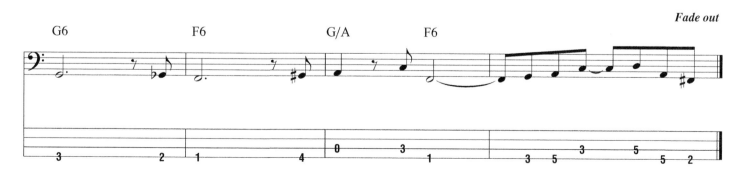

Do It Again

Words and Music by Walter Becker and Donald Fagen

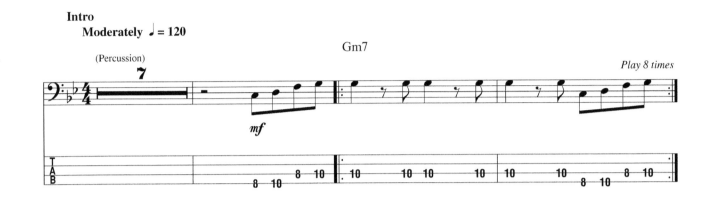

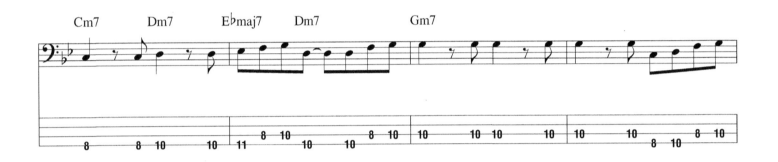

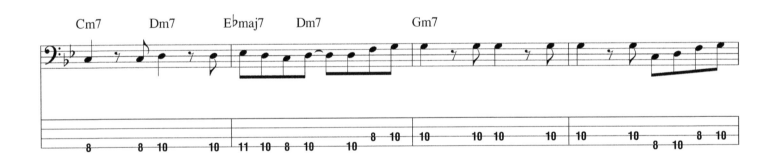

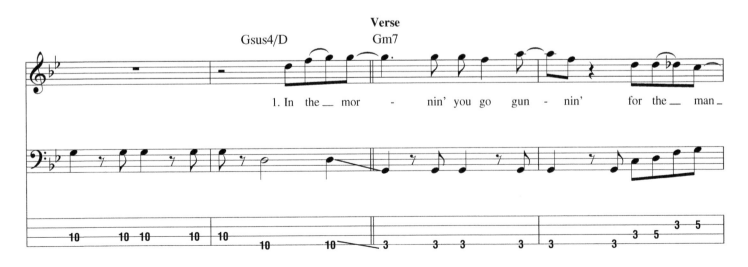

1. In the __ mor - nin' you go gun - nin' for the __ man __

Interlude

Verse

a lit-tle wild __ one and she brings __ you on-ly sor - row. __ All the __ time __

__ you know she's smil - in'. You'll be __ on __ your knees __ to-mor - row. Yeah, __ you go

Chorus

Cm7/G   Dm7   E♭maj7   Dm7   Gm7

back,   Jack,   do it a - gain, _____ wheel turn - in' 'round __

Cm7   Dm7   E♭maj7   Dm7

__ and 'round. __ You go __ back,   Jack,   do it a - gain. _____

Elec. Sitar Solo

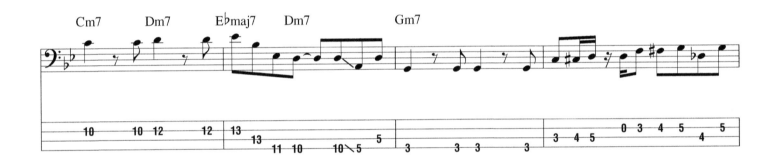

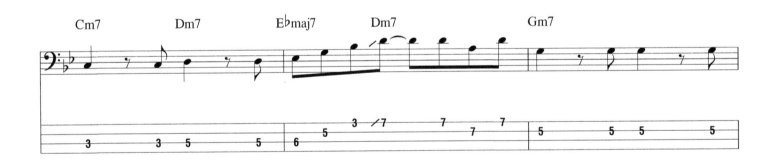

Organic Solo

Chorus

Cm7　　Dm7　　E♭maj7　　Dm7

____ them on __ the ta - ble. Yeah, _ you go back, Jack, do it a - gain, _____

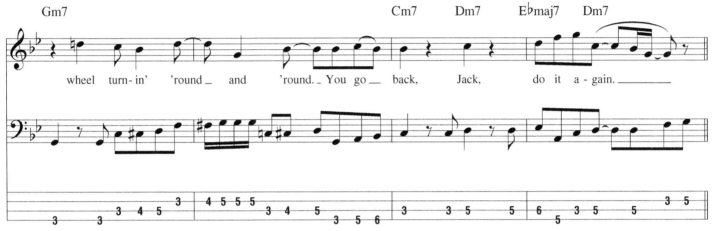

Gm7　　　　　　　　　　Cm7　　Dm7　　E♭maj7　　Dm7

wheel turn- in' 'round _ and 'round. _ You go _ back, Jack, do it a - gain. _____

Outro-Guitar Solo

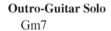

Gm7

Begin fade

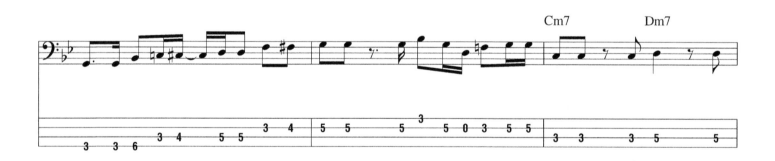

Fade out

FM

from the film FM

Words and Music by Walter Becker and Donald Fagen

F - M. No stat - ic at all. _____

Interlude

Saxophone Solo

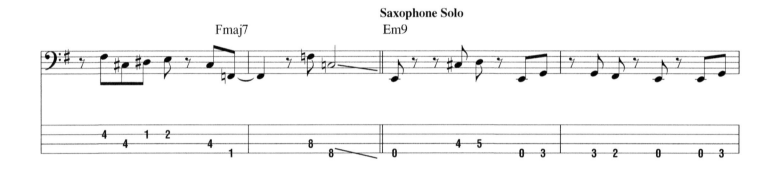

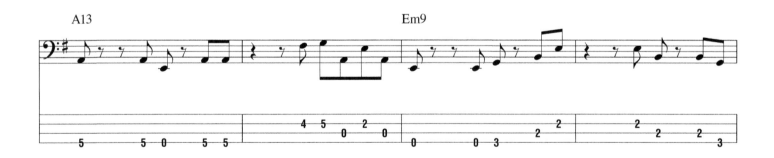

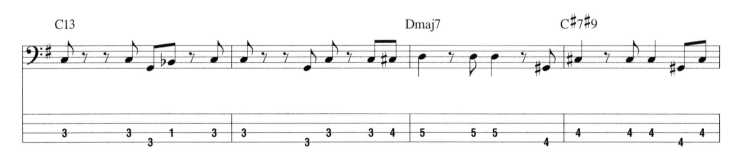

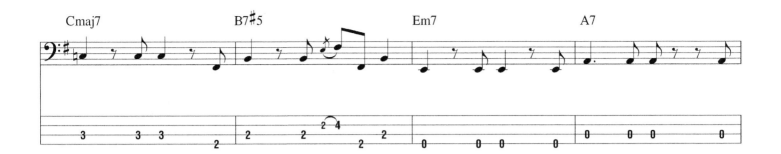

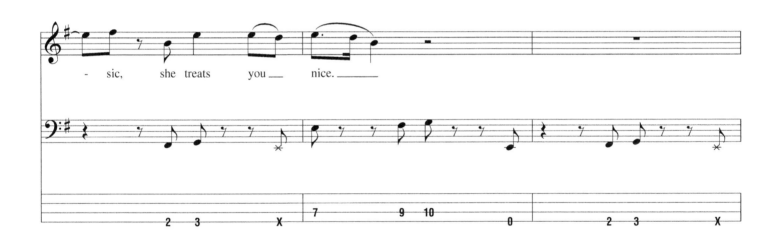

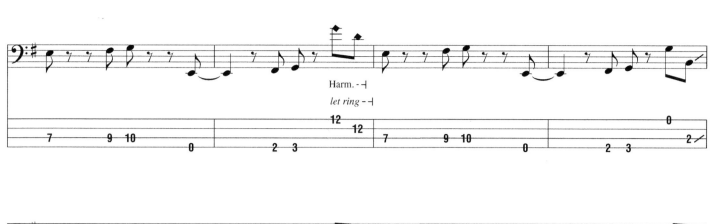

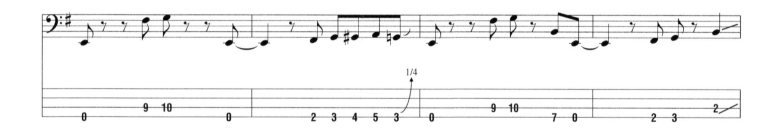

Begin fade

Repeat and fade

Hey Nineteen

Words and Music by Walter Becker and Donald Fagen

Josie

Words and Music by Walter Becker and Donald Fagen

Bridge

N.C.

F#7#9   B7#9

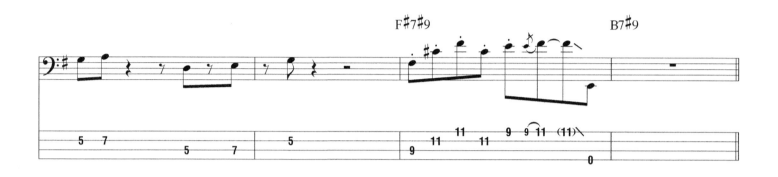

Guitar Solo

Em7

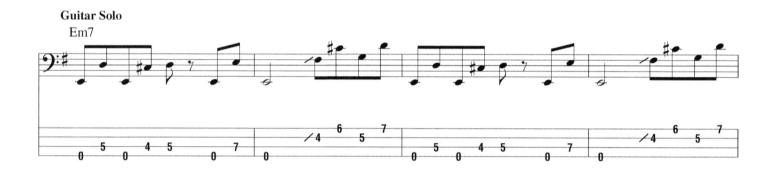

A/D   G/C   D/G   C/F

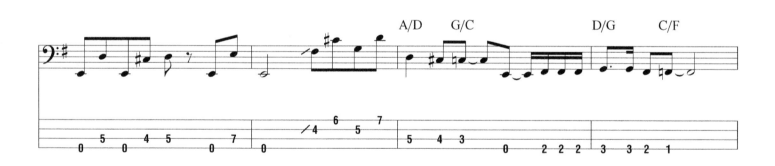

Em7   A7   G/C D/G C/F

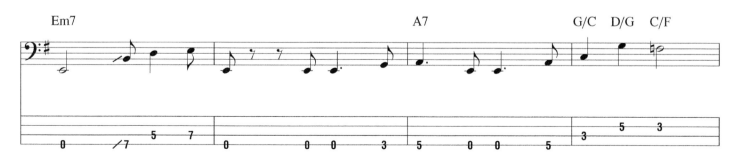

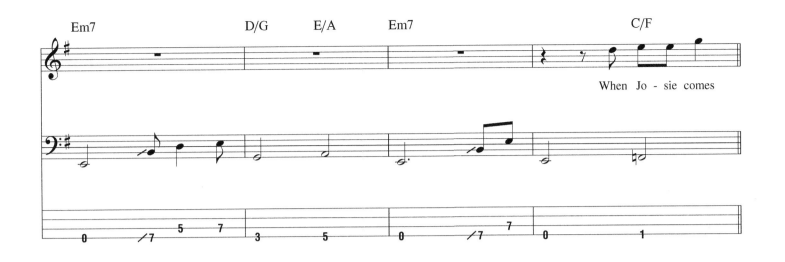

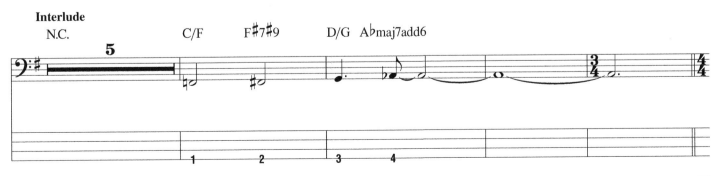

Outro

Em7

Begin fade

Play 4 times

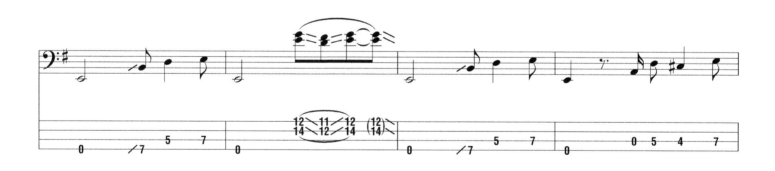

Fade out

Rikki Don't Lose That Number

Words and Music by Walter Becker and Donald Fagen

*Key signature denotes E Mixolydian.

Fill 1

D.S. al Coda

⊕ Coda

home.

Guitar Solo

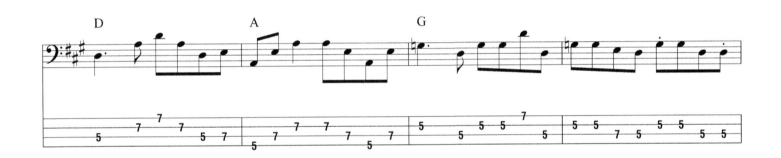

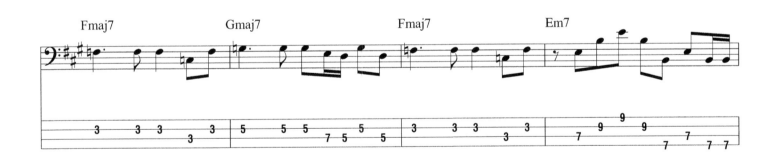

Additional Lyrics

2. I have a friend in town, he's heard your name.
We can go out driving on Slow Hand-Row.
We could stay inside and play games, I don't know.
And you could have a change of heart.

Reeling in the Years

Words and Music by Walter Becker and Donald Fagen

*Key signature denotes A Mixolydian.

Outro

Additional Lyrics

2. You've been tellin' me you're a genius since you were seventeen.
   In all the time I've known you I still don't know what you mean.
   The weekend at the college didn't turn out like you planned.
   The things that pass for knowledge I can't understand.

3. I've spent a lot of money and I've spent a lot of time.
   The trip we made to Hollywood is etched upon my mind.
   After all the things we've done and seen you find another man.
   The things you think are useless I can't understand.

Hal•Leonard®
BASS
PLAY-ALONG

The Bass Play-Along™ Series will help you play your favorite songs quickly and easily! Just follow the tab, listen to the audio to hear how the bass should sound, and then play-along using the separate backing tracks. The melody and lyrics are also included in the book in case you want to sing, or to simply help you follow along. The audio files are enhanced so you can adjust the recording to any tempo without changing pitch!

1. Rock
00699674 Book/Online Audio $16.99

2. R&B
00699675 Book/Online Audio $16.99

3. Songs for Beginners
00346426 Book/Online Audio $16.99

4. '90s Rock
00294992 Book/Online Audio $16.99

5. Funk
00699680 Book/Online Audio $16.99

6. Classic Rock
00699678 Book/Online Audio $17.99

8. Punk Rock
00699813 Book/CD Pack $12.95

9. Blues
00699817 Book/Online Audio.......................................$16.99

10. Jimi Hendrix – Smash Hits
00699815 Book/Online Audio.......................................$17.99

11. Country
00699818 Book/CD Pack $12.95

12. Punk Classics
00699814 Book/CD Pack $12.99

13. The Beatles
00275504 Book/Online Audio $17.99

14. Modern Rock
00699821 Book/CD Pack...$14.99

15. Mainstream Rock
00699822 Book/CD Pack...$14.99

16. '80s Metal
00699825 Book/CD Pack...$16.99

17. Pop Metal
00699826 Book/CD Pack...$14.99

18. Blues Rock
00699828 Book/CD Pack...$19.99

19. Steely Dan
00700203 Book/Online Audio $17.99

20. The Police
00700270 Book/Online Audio $19.99

21. Metallica: 1983-1988
00234338 Book/Online Audio $19.99

22. Metallica: 1991-2016
00234339 Book/Online Audio $19.99

23. Pink Floyd – Dark Side of The Moon
00700847 Book/Online Audio $16.99

24. Weezer
00700960 Book/CD Pack $17.99

25. Nirvana
00701047 Book/Online Audio $17.99

26. Black Sabbath
00701180 Book/Online Audio $17.99

27. Kiss
00701181 Book/Online Audio.......................................$17.99

28. The Who
00701182 Book/Online Audio $19.99

29. Eric Clapton
00701183 Book/Online Audio $17.99

30. Early Rock
00701184 Book/CD Pack $15.99

31. The 1970s
00701185 Book/CD Pack $14.99

32. Cover Band Hits
00211598 Book/Online Audio $16.99

33. Christmas Hits
00701197 Book/CD Pack $12.99

34. Easy Songs
00701480 Book/Online Audio $17.99

35. Bob Marley
00701702 Book/Online Audio $17.99

36. Aerosmith
00701886 Book/CD Pack...$14.99

37. Modern Worship
00701920 Book/Online Audio $19.99

38. Avenged Sevenfold
00702386 Book/CD Pack $16.99

39. Queen
00702387 Book/Online Audio $17.99

40. AC/DC
14041594 Book/Online Audio $17.99

41. U2
00702582 Book/Online Audio.......................................$19.99

42. Red Hot Chili Peppers
00702991 Book/Online Audio.......................................$19.99

43. Paul McCartney
00703079 Book/Online Audio.......................................$19.99

44. Megadeth
00703080 Book/CD Pack...$16.99

45. Slipknot
00703201 Book/CD Pack $17.99

46. Best Bass Lines Ever
00103359 Book/Online Audio.......................................$19.99

47. Dream Theater
00111940 Book/Online Audio $24.99

48. James Brown
00117421 Book/CD Pack...$16.99

49. Eagles
00119936 Book/Online Audio.......................................$17.99

50. Jaco Pastorius
00128407 Book/Online Audio.......................................$17.99

51. Stevie Ray Vaughan
00146154 Book/CD Pack...$16.99

52. Cream
00146159 Book/Online Audio $19.99

56. Bob Seger
00275503 Book/Online Audio.......................................$16.99

57. Iron Maiden
00278398 Book/Online Audio.......................................$17.99

58. Southern Rock
00278436 Book/Online Audio.......................................$17.99

Hal•Leonard®

Visit Hal Leonard Online at **www.halleonard.com**

BASS RECORDED VERSIONS

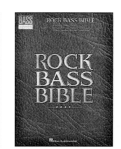

Bass Recorded Versions feature authentic transcriptions written in standard notation and tablature for bass guitar. This series features complete bass lines from the classics to contemporary superstars.

25 Essential Rock Bass Classics
00690210 / $19.99

Avenged Sevenfold – Nightmare
00691054 / $19.99

The Beatles – Abbey Road
00128336 / $24.99

The Beatles – 1962-1966
00690556 / $19.99

The Beatles – 1967-1970
00690557 / $24.99

Best of Bass Tab
00141806 / $17.99

The Best of Blink 182
00690549 / $18.99

Blues Bass Classics
00690291 / $22.99

Boston – Bass Collection
00690935 / $19.95

Stanley Clarke – Collection
00672307 / $22.99

Dream Theater – Bass Anthology
00119345 / $29.99

Funk Bass Bible
00690744 / $27.99

Hard Rock Bass Bible
00690746 / $22.99

Jimi Hendrix – Are You Experienced?
00690371 / $17.95

Jimi Hendrix – Bass Tab Collection
00160505 / $24.99

Iron Maiden – Bass Anthology
00690867 / $24.99

Jazz Bass Classics
00102070 / $19.99

The Best of Kiss
00690080 / $22.99

Lynyrd Skynyrd – All-Time Greatest Hits
00690956 / $24.99

Bob Marley – Bass Collection
00690568 / $24.99

Mastodon – Crack the Skye
00691007 / $19.99

Megadeth – Bass Anthology
00691191 / $22.99

Metal Bass Tabs
00103358 / $22.99

Best of Marcus Miller
00690811 / $29.99

Motown Bass Classics
00690253 / $19.99

Muse – Bass Tab Collection
00123275 / $22.99

Nirvana – Bass Collection
00690066 / $19.99

Nothing More – Guitar & Bass Collection
00265439 / $24.99

The Offspring – Greatest Hits
00690809 / $17.95

The Essential Jaco Pastorius
00690420 / $22.99

Jaco Pastorius – Greatest Jazz Fusion Bass Player
00690421 / $24.99

Pearl Jam – Ten
00694882 / $22.99

Pink Floyd – Dark Side of the Moon
00660172 / $19.99

The Best of Police
00660207 / $24.99

Pop/Rock Bass Bible
00690747 / $24.99

Queen – The Bass Collection
00690065 / $22.99

R&B Bass Bible
00690745 / $24.99

Rage Against the Machine
00690248 / $22.99

Red Hot Chili Peppers – BloodSugarSexMagik
00690064 / $22.99

Red Hot Chili Peppers – By the Way
00690585 / $24.99

Red Hot Chili Peppers – Californication
00690390 / $22.99

Red Hot Chili Peppers – Greatest Hits
00690675 / $22.99

Red Hot Chili Peppers – I'm with You
00691167 / $22.99

Red Hot Chili Peppers – One Hot Minute
00690091 / $22.99

Red Hot Chili Peppers – Stadium Arcadium
00690853 / Book Only $24.95

Rock Bass Bible
00690446 / $22.99

Rolling Stones – Bass Collection
00690256 / $24.99

Royal Blood
00151826 / $24.99

Rush – The Spirit of Radio: Greatest Hits 1974-1987
00323856 / $24.99

Best of Billy Sheehan
00173972 / $24.99

Slap Bass Bible
00159716 / $29.99

Sly & The Family Stone for Bass
00109733 / $24.99

Best of Yes
00103044 / $24.99

Best of ZZ Top for Bass
00691069 / $24.99

Visit Hal Leonard Online at
www.halleonard.com

Prices, contents & availability subject to change without notice.
Some products may not be available outside the U.S.A.

BASS BUILDERS

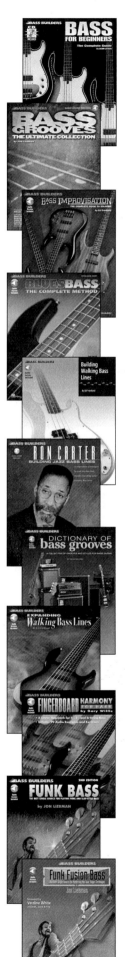

A series of technique book/audio packages created for the purposeful building and development of your chops. Each volume is written by an expert in that particular technique. And with the inclusion of audio, the added dimension of hearing exactly how to play particular grooves and techniques make these truly like private lessons.

BASS FOR BEGINNERS
by Glenn Letsch
00695099 Book/CD Pack...$19.95

BASS GROOVES
by Jon Liebman
00696028 Book/Online Audio $19.99

BASS IMPROVISATION
by Ed Friedland
00695164 Book/Online Audio $19.99

BLUES BASS
by Jon Liebman
00695235 Book/Online Audio $19.99

BUILDING WALKING BASS LINES
by Ed Friedland
00695008 Book/Online Audio $19.99

**RON CARTER –
BUILDING JAZZ BASS LINES**
00841240 Book/Online Audio $19.99

DICTIONARY OF BASS GROOVES
by Sean Malone
00695266 Book/Online Audio $14.95

EXPANDING WALKING BASS LINES
by Ed Friedland
00695026 Book/Online Audio $19.99

FINGERBOARD HARMONY FOR BASS
by Gary Willis
00695043 Book/Online Audio $17.99

FUNK BASS
by Jon Liebman
00699348 Book/Online Audio $19.99

FUNK/FUSION BASS
by Jon Liebman
00696553 Book/Online Audio $24.99

HIP-HOP BASS
by Josquin des Prés
00695589 Book/Online Audio $15.99

JAZZ BASS
by Ed Friedland
00695084 Book/Online Audio $17.99

**JERRY JEMMOTT –
BLUES AND RHYTHM &
BLUES BASS TECHNIQUE**
00695176 Book/CD Pack...$24.99

JUMP 'N' BLUES BASS
by Keith Rosier
00695292 Book/Online Audio $17.99

THE LOST ART OF COUNTRY BASS
by Keith Rosier
00695107 Book/Online Audio $19.99

PENTATONIC SCALES FOR BASS
by Ed Friedland
00696224 Book/Online Audio $19.99

REGGAE BASS
by Ed Friedland
00695163 Book/Online Audio $16.99

'70S FUNK & DISCO BASS
by Josquin des Prés
00695614 Book/Online Audio $16.99

**SIMPLIFIED SIGHT-READING
FOR BASS**
by Josquin des Prés
00695085 Book/Online Audio $17.99

6-STRING BASSICS
by David Gross
00695221 Book/Online Audio $14.99

HAL•LEONARD®

halleonard.com

Prices, contents and availability subject to change without notice; All prices are listed in U.S. funds